# CHER BIOGRAPHY

The Emergence Cherilyn Sarkisian

Sekani Jakes

Copyright © 2024 by Sekani Jakes All rights reserved. No part of this book may be used or reproduced in any form without written permission, except in the case of brief quotations embodied in critical articles or reviews. Printed in the United States of America.

# CONTENT

1 CHAPTER ONE.................................................................

2 CHAPTER TWO.................................................................

3 CHAPTER THREE...............................................................

4 CHAPTER FOUR................................................................

5 CHAPTER FIVE................................................................

6 CHAPTER SIX.................................................................

7 THE END.....................................................................

CHER

# Chapter One

**The Making of Cher**

"Someone once asked me why I'm doing all this, and I said because there'll come a day where I can't," Cher reflected with her characteristic honesty. "I want to make sure that I don't think, 'If only I'd done that one thing. If only I'd tried.' It's not about desperation—it's knowing that I won't always be able to." These words encapsulate her philosophy: a relentless drive to seize life's opportunities while she can.

Cher's story is a proof of resilience—a quintessential tale of a girl who transformed adversity into triumph. Her beginnings, however, were starkly different from the glamour and adoration that would define her later years.

On the 20th of May(46), Cherilyn Sarkisian was birthed in El-Centro. A truck driver named John Sarkisian, who haa history of gambling and drug abuse, and a teenage actress named Georgia Holt. Their rocky marriage ended not long after Cher was born. Just out of her teenage years and freshly unmarried, Georgia felt the shackles of cultural pressure and financial hardship. She was placed in a Catholic foster home for a short and traumatic period, and the event left emotional scars.

The question "Where do I belong?" lingered throughout her formative years. Her mother's marital status had changed multiple times by the time she reached the age of ten. As the only child in her family with dark hair, Cher frequently felt like an outsider, even though Georgia's affection for her was unfaltering. "I was dyslexic—well, I am dyslexic," Cher revealed afterwards. Because I had trouble seeing numbers and reading, it was a major challenge for me when I was a kid. Whatever, my mom would always tell me. That's brilliant. As an artist, she always made sure I never doubted myself. Her faith in me was unwavering. Despite her own hardships, Cher's mother was an enduring source of strength and inspiration for her daughter. Even though Georgia's ambitions to become famous were never realized, they did inspire her daughter to follow in her footsteps. Singing around the home, they would harmonize their voices with the sounds of their simple lives.

**A Rough Start in L.A.**

Cher's childhood was marked by financial hardship. She vividly recalled, "My grandmother picked cotton with my mother. It was a rough life. There was a time when I lost the soles of my shoes and had to use rubber bands to keep them on. Walking to school like that—I'll never forget it. Those experiences shaped me. I want people to have better lives, to feel good about themselves, and to have access to decent schools—not just for the rich."

Georgia's unwavering determination to make ends meet left an indelible mark on young Cher. Her mother's resilience inspired her to reject the word "no." "No is just some stupid word someone made up," Cher would later declare. "I've tanked. I've gotten huge losses & even big successes. But those losses make you wanna keep going."

**Dreams Sparked by the Silver Screen**

Her upbringing in Los Angeles exposed her to the glitter of Hollywood. She looked up to strong female performers like Hepburn, Bette, and Dietrich. Still, the blonde, fair-skinned beauty ideal that predominated on film was something she had a hard time seeing in herself. Models, actors, and singers were all blonde when I was a kid. "I had dark hair and eyes and was the very first female on Vogue," she said. "Back that time that was a huge deal." The 50s' very specific standards for beauty only served to heighten her self-esteem issues. Her defiant nature, though, started to show. She became known for her signature large sunglasses, which she got from Audrey Hepburn. She was expelled from school for refusing to remove them when asked to do so. Cher's defiance extended beyond her wardrobe. At thirteen, she started driving and cruised the streets of LA in stolen moments of freedom. At fourteen years old, she was admonished by the police for her reckless behaviors.

But these defiances showed that she was a young woman who was hell-bent on making her own way. Unexpectedly, she had her first encounter with the music industry. She was asked to fill in as a backup vocalist when one of the artists didn't show up while she was loitering around LA music studios. Even though it was a small chance encounter, it ignited a spark—the idea that music may be her calling.

## A Fateful Encounter

Changes that would alter her life's trajectory occurred in November 1962. The twenty-seven-year-old musician and record promoter Bono was her double date when she was sixteen years old. Even though she had another date, Sonny was the one who really caught her eye. Right after they met, they hit it off, and Cher took him up on his offer to be his housekeeper once her roommate left. They had a rapid blossoming of their personal and professional partnership.

"I met Sonny when I was born in Los Angeles," Cher reflected afterwards. Sonny interjected, saying, "I've been in the business for a lot longer than her". We both wanted to be in the music industry, and she was my biggest influence. It was effortless. She was able to establish herself as a successful musician with Bono's guidance. A cause of insecurity for her as a child, her deep contralto voice eventually became her distinctive signature. Love You...Ringo, her debut track, was a bust because Disk Jockey(s) kept thinking her voice was that of a man. The indisputable chemistry between Bono and Cher persisted despite the setback.

Initially performing under the moniker Caesar-Cleo, the pair worked hard to gain momentum. It wasn't until they rebranded as Sunny&Cher in 1965 that their fortunes began to change. On the advice of the Rolling Stones, they traveled to the United Kingdom, where their eccentric fashion and unconventional style caused a sensation. The press took notice of Cher's self-designed clothes, which featured bell bottoms and fur vests.

They were kicked out of the Hilton for their outrageously eccentric outfits, but the backlash only served to increase the couple's already meteoric climb to fame. What Cher meant was that the group couldn't be categorized as mod, rocker, or anything else. "Yet we reaped its benefits."

## The Breakthrough

In '65, With the publication of their 1st album, the duo introduced the world to their signature tune., Got You Babe...anthem of love & partnership rocketed to the top of the charts in America, UK, and even Canada. Its feel-good vibe resonated with a generation seeking an escape from societal turmoil. The duo reached new heights thanks to the music's spectacular success. Having five tracks in the Top fifty at the same time is an accomplishment that has only been accomplished by Presley & The Beatles. Their music and image cemented their place as icons of the 60s counterculture.

## Her Vision Beyond the Spotlight

Despite her newfound fame, Cher never forgot her roots or the struggles of her youth. "My mom used to say, 'I was complaining about having no shoes until I saw the man who had no feet,'" she shared. "That stuck with me. It's about counting your blessings and giving back. I've instilled that in my children."

Her career has been propelled by her unwavering commitment to uplifting others. She stressed that her goal was for people to have a positive self-image. Everyone, not just the wealthy, should have access to decent schools, in my opinion. The pilgrimage of Little Sarkisian from a dyslexic, insecure lassie to one half of an international sensation is a story of perseverance and self-belief. Her determination to defy expectations—whether in fashion, music, or life—set the stage for a career that would span decades and inspire generations.

As Cher herself put it, "I've had great successes and huge losses, but I keep going. I want everyone, especially women, to know that they don't have to take 'no' for an answer. No is just

a word, and we can rise above it."

# Chapter Two

### Highs & Lows - Fame & Fracture

By 1967, the couple had achieved monumental success, selling over 40m tracks globally. Their hits like Got You Babe...had captured the spirit of that era, symbolizing love & partnership. The changing cultural climate of the 1960s, however, started to put strain on their relationship and careers. Their stereotypically monogamous persona appeared at odds with the liberated spirit of the Sexual Revolution. Sonny refused to budge from their original formula, unmoved by the shifting tides of popular music. The pair produced Good Times, a film, in an effort to reinvigorate their careers. It was her big screen debut, and despite the project's best efforts, it failed to live up to expectations. The film's box office bomb cast doubt on their capacity to succeed as a creative team, and she began to distrust herself. Mr. Bono was not pleased with her decision to pursue a solo music endeavor, but she persisted nevertheless.

She found a new creative voice through her own work, but tensions in her connection with Sonny were growing. Their once-inseparable dynamic now appeared to be working against them due to his domineering influence over her profession and suspicions of infidelity. Amidst all the drama, they nevertheless got engaged and promised one other a wonderful family life. She delivered their little girl, Chastity, in 69, and the pair was married not long after.

**Speaking on the Power Couple's Success**
During a candid interview, she reflected on their enduring appeal:
> "I don't know, it just happened. It's just timing and talent, I think. And, uh..."

Sonny, ever analytical, shared his take:

> "I think it's a combination of things. Timing, of course, is very important. And then, the fact that we're a married couple has a big bearing on our success because kids see us as a symbol of love. They like our music, the way we dress—it's colorful, and it's us."

However, Sonny's nostalgia for their image as a wholesome pair became a double-edged sword. His unwillingness to modernize alienated younger audiences.

**The Gamble That Backfired**

In a bold move, the couple decided to produce another film, Chastity, named after their daughter. The art film, directed by Sonny, was meant to explore existential themes. Instead, it flopped disastrously, plunging them into financial ruin. The failure was a wake-up call. To recover, they pivoted to live performances, tailoring their nightclub routine for a more mature audience.

Unexpectedly, moving to live performances was a game-changer. At first, they were heckled, which was discouraging but eventually turned into a chance to succeed. The duo began incorporating witty comebacks, pivoting the heckles into a comedic highlight of their performances. Television executives took notice, resulting in the creation of The S&C Comedy Hour in '71.

**Her Bold Fashion Statements**

The show wasn't just about humor—it became a platform for her to express herself in ways she hadn't before. Her daring fashion choices, often designed by Bob Mackie, pushed the boundaries of television's conservative standards.

> "My clothes were shocking, you know? What I wore was really shocking. But I was going to wear what I wanted. If my

audience didn't like it, I would know. Audiences will tell you what they think, so I just didn't care. You're going to tell me what I can do? I don't think so," Cher later recalled.

One particularly iconic moment was the exposure of her belly button—a first for television. This small but defiant act of self-expression symbolized the breaking of rigid societal norms.

> "These girls today are pushing the envelope. Back then, I was doing the same thing. It's about self-expression, which is what artists do. I think we knocked down some walls, but there are still more walls to be broken ," she said.

Her fearlessness set the path for artists of the future to have unrestricted creative freedom.

**Crackles Beneath the Glittering Surface**

Despite the outward success of their TV show, rumors of her husband's infidelity began to surface. For Cherilyn, the betrayal cut deep. The final straw in their marriage came when she discovered he had been cheating on her. The two kept working together on the show, though, because it benefited their logo. While their typical sarcastic digs at Sonny became an integral part of their humor, their distance was widening behind the scenes. She pursued a solo career because she was hell-bent on finding her own path.

She finally broke through with Thieves, Tramps, and Gypsies. The sensual music video, which featured her in a gypsy-inspired outfit, completely destroyed her reputation as someone who was suitable for families. The song tackled controversial topics like racism, prostitution, and teenage pregnancy, showcasing her ability to confront social issues head-on.

Her subsequent smash single, Half-Breed, cemented her autonomy even more. Cher sang about the challenges of multiracial identity while dressing as a proud Cherokee woman and riding a horse. She proved she could succeed without Sonny with this song, which became her subsequent solo US number one.

**A Bitter Divorce**

The year 1974 was the year she finally snapped. The breaking point came when she learned that Mr. Bono had set up Cher Enterprises in a manner that practically gave her nothing. In a daring and uncommon action, she sought a divorce, claiming involuntary slavery as her grounds. The end of her marriage and the onset of her path as a fully independent woman were both signified by the disintegration of their union.

## Reinvention Through Disco

As the 1970s drew to a close, Cher re-evaluated her musical direction. She ventured into disco, a genre that was both glamorous and bold, much like her. Her album Take Me Home marked a triumphant return to the charts. Bob Mackie's dazzling costumes added a layer of theatricality to her performances, perfectly complementing the pulsating beats of disco.

Cher's willingness to reinvent herself paid off once again, but she soon pivoted, this time forming a rock band, Black Rose. The move surprised both fans and critics.

## Cher on Her Rock Aspirations

In an interview, Cher addressed the skepticism surrounding her rock transformation:
> "People are always resistant to new ideas. Half the people I talk to think it's a good idea, and half don't. But it's something

I want to do. If people eventually like it, they will. And if they don't, they won't."

Though Black Rose didn't achieve commercial success, the project was a testament to Cher's unyielding desire to follow her passions.

**Fighting for Women's Rights**

The early 1980s saw Cher doubling down on her advocacy for women's rights. The sexism she encountered in Hollywood fueled her determination to speak out.

> "We've had to fight for everything we've gotten. If you ask for the same things on a set that a man asks for, you're labeled difficult. It's not fair. Women have to work twice as hard to be taken seriously," she said.

Cher's candor and resilience inspired a new generation of women to demand equality in their careers and personal lives.

**Looking Ahead**

By the end of this chapter, Cher had firmly established herself as more than just Sonny's other half. She was a trailblazer in music, fashion, and feminism, breaking barriers and redefining what it meant to be a woman in the entertainment industry. Though the road was fraught with challenges, Cher emerged stronger, wiser, and ready to conquer whatever lay ahead.

# Chapter Three

**The Actress Behind the Stardom**

The 1980s marked a transformative period for Cher, as she turned her focus from music to cinema. Breaking barriers as both an artist and a woman, she faced relentless challenges while carving her path into Hollywood. This chapter delves into her journey, revealing her struggles, triumphs, and the captivating persona that made her an icon.

Cher described her foray into acting with candor: "I'm really happy with what I'm doing. And if I got an award or a nomination, it would make it better. If I don't, well... it's fine." Yet, as her career trajectory would soon prove, Cher's acting was far from just "fine." Her transition from pop singer to serious actress not only redefined her career but also reshaped public perception of her talent.

**From Glitter to Gold**

In 1987, Cher achieved a breakthrough with her role in Moonstruck, a romantic comedy-drama where her portrayal of Loretta Castorini earned widespread acclaim. During an interview following her Golden Globe win for the role, Cher's emotions were as striking as her words.

Interviewer: "You've won for Moonstruck. How do you feel?"

Cher: "I feel fabulous. I feel really great."

Her genuine joy masked the years of struggle it had taken to reach that moment. Reflecting on her journey, Cher admitted, "It's been really a difficult struggle to get here. At the beginning of this road, every person in that audience was someone who wouldn't have given much hope. If I were a patient on a sick list, I probably would have died. Achieving something that seemed so impossible feels incredible."

The following months brought even greater acclaim as Cher won the Academy Award for Best Actress. She stood on the world's most prestigious stage, thanking her supporters and acknowledging her mother for teaching her to persevere.

Interviewer: "What does this win mean to you personally?"

Cher: "It means everything. To stand here and know the struggles that brought me here—it's overwhelming. This isn't just my win; it's for everyone who believed in me when it seemed impossible."

Her victory symbolized more than just professional achievement—it was a cultural moment. Cher had shattered stereotypes, proving that women in their 40s could thrive in Hollywood, and that a singer could excel as a serious actress.

**The Many Faces of Cher**

Despite her accolades, Cher remained enigmatic. Rumors about her on-set demeanor fueled curiosity. When asked if she was "difficult" or "sweet," she laughed and quipped, "Yes."

For Cher, acting was about authenticity. "I like playing regular people so others don't feel alone in the world. I want to inspire people by showing that hardships can be overcome."

Balancing career and motherhood proved equally challenging. Cher described her whirlwind life: "A career, two households, construction work in New York—it's a lot. One night, I thought I'd finally get a good night's sleep. Then, at 2:30 a.m., Elijah [her son] came downstairs with a fever of 102.5. I stayed up with him until he fell asleep at 4:30, then got up at 9:00 for an interview. Sometimes I feel like that goddess with a thousand arms, juggling everything and not doing a great job at any of it."

Her candidness endeared her to fans, who saw not just a star but a relatable woman navigating life's complexities.

**A Bold Comeback**

In 1989, Cher's 19th solo album, Heart of Stone, marked her triumphant return to music. The album's hit single, If I Could Turn Back Time, thrust her back into the spotlight—but not without controversy.

Filming the song's music video aboard the USS Missouri, Cher wore a provocative black fishnet bodysuit, paired with a leather jacket. While the Navy had authorized the shoot, her daring outfit—and her decision to straddle a cannon—caught them off guard. The Secretary of the Navy even considered firing the ship's captain for approving the spectacle. Despite the backlash, Cher remained unapologetic. "I've always been bold," she said. "I think people know that I'm trying. I work hard and survive, and that's what people like about me."

The video's controversy didn't deter its success. While some networks refused to air it, the song climbed the charts and earned Cher a People's Choice Award that same year.

**A Multifaceted Legacy**

By the end of the decade, Cher had conquered music, film, and television. Yet, she remained as grounded as ever.

Interviewer: "What's left for you to accomplish?"

Cher: "I'm going to become a marine biologist," she joked, before adding thoughtfully, "Success isn't about ticking off boxes. It's about expression. I haven't always been successful in everything I've attempted, but I've been able to express myself, and that's what matters."

When asked about her motivations, Cher responded with characteristic wit: "We're working girls. Everybody has to work. For me, it's about emotion, artistry—and, of course, the money."

Cher's ability to balance humor with heartfelt insight made her a singular presence in Hollywood. Her journey wasn't just about personal triumph—it was about inspiring others to embrace their individuality and persevere through challenges.

**Conclusion**

As Cher closed the 1980s, she stood as a symbol of resilience and reinvention. Her journey from pop singer to Academy Award-winning actress defied the odds, breaking barriers for women in entertainment. Through it all, she remained unapologetically herself—a daring, dazzling icon whose story continues to inspire.

# Chapter Four

**Chaz's Transition and Cher's Journey of Acceptance**

Chaz Bono, born Chastity Bono in 1969, made headlines in 1995 when he publicly came out as gay. This brave declaration marked the beginning of an extraordinary journey, one that would eventually see him reveal in 2009 that he was transgender. Cher, a global icon and Chaz's mother, navigated the complex emotions of acceptance and adaptation, sharing her experience with raw honesty and love.

**Chaz's Courageous Journey**

During an interview shortly after stepping down from GLAAD, Chaz reflected on a moment of personal reinvention, saying:

"Uh, um, I'm not doing anything right now. I just left GLAAD, and I, um, I'm taking some time off and, uh, going to reinvent myself."

Chaz's openness inspired many, but it also required significant inner strength to address societal stigma. His 2011 documentary, Becoming Chaz, offered an intimate look at his gender reassignment process. Chaz explained:

"I'm doing this because I want to try to help people, you know? I want to put a face on an issue that people don't understand. That's why I did this publicly."

**Cher's Initial Struggles and Growth**

Cher, known for her fierce independence and resilience, admitted to struggling when Chaz first came out as gay and later as transgender. She candidly described her feelings:

"It was a little bit difficult but not as difficult as finding out that Chaz was gay. I mean, I had friends with like a billion gay people, but until you go through it with your child...you realize you have lost your child. That's a kind of strange thing—to feel like the child that you know is a new child you have to get to know."

Her honesty highlighted the emotional complexity of the experience. She continued:

"I started to really enjoy that process, but you have to take some little baby steps before you can go, 'Yes, I feel totally comfortable with this.'"

## Health Concerns and Protective Instincts

Cher's resistance to Chaz's transition wasn't about identity but about concern for his health. Speaking about her apprehensions, she said:

"I'm afraid he's not going to be healthy. I'm afraid it's too much for him. I worry about the drugs he has to take to keep this. I don't know that much about it, but I want to make sure that whatever it is, it's not going to hurt him."

Despite these worries, Cher empathized deeply with Chaz's perspective:

"Imagine waking up tomorrow and you're not the sex you went to bed as last night. What would you do? How would you feel? I understand why he said, 'This is not me. I don't want to live this way.'"

**Cher's Unwavering Love and Advocacy**

As Chaz navigated his transformation, Cher became a steadfast ally. Over time, her perspective evolved, and her love for Chaz transcended any initial fears. She came to understand and celebrate his authenticity, offering a poignant example of a parent's unconditional love.

Cher's journey mirrored her resilience in the face of other personal tragedies, such as the death of Sonny Bono in 1998. Sonny, her former husband and longtime musical partner, died in a skiing accident, leaving a void in her life. In a tearful eulogy, Cher said:

"Bono is, without a doubt, the most memorable character I have ever encountered. That person remains Sonny to me, regardless of the duration I remain or who I meet."

## Rising Above Challenges

Despite personal losses, Cher continued to break barriers in her career and personal life. The late 1990s saw her recognized for her contributions to the entertainment industry, cementing her place as a Hollywood legend with a star on the Walk of Fame. Yet, Cher's greatest pride remained her children. When asked about her most significant life moments, she replied:

"The biggest two moments in my life were my kids. This could be the third biggest moment of my life."

## Reinvention Through Music

True to her reputation for reinvention, Cher revolutionized the music industry in 1998 with Believe, a dance-pop anthem that introduced the world to autotune as an artistic effect. Reflecting on its impact, she remarked:

"I don't think anybody could have anticipated the reaction. It was crazy. Every night, I'd come out on stage thinking, 'What are these people doing here?'"

The song became a global phenomenon, cementing Cher's status as a pop culture icon. Its message of empowerment resonated deeply, much like Chaz's journey toward self-discovery and acceptance.

## Philanthropy and Advocacy

Away from the spotlight, Cher channeled her energy into humanitarian work. One of her most notable projects was building a school in Kenya, a cause she took on after seeing the struggles of local children. She recalled:

"I was in bed watching this couple from Scotland who stumbled upon kids trying to study in shacks. I just thought, 'This is terrible.' I called an Englishman who had built structures there, and we created a beautiful school."

Cher's philosophy of taking action resonated with her audience:

"I believe what comes to you belongs to you. If something happens to you and you're engaged in it, then it's your duty to do something about it."

**Legacy of Love and Acceptance**

Cher's journey with Chaz epitomized her resilience, empathy, and courage. As she supported her child's transition, she also redefined motherhood, demonstrating that love could triumph over fear and misunderstanding. Her own words encapsulated this transformation:

"I was always myself. I just had to find another way to expose who I was."

Chaz's courage and Cher's unwavering support created a powerful narrative of authenticity and acceptance, inspiring countless families navigating similar journeys. Cher's legacy, shaped by reinvention and resilience, became even richer through her profound role as a mother.

# Chapter Five

**A Voice of Defiance in Tumultuous Times**

Cher's political engagement grew out of the turbulent landscape of the early 21st century, where her outspokenness became a defining trait. She viewed the Bush presidency as a divisive period and expressed frustration over what she perceived as a lack of leadership. "As far as I can tell, [Bush] just thinks we're going to be in this terrorist war forever," she remarked, critiquing the administration's policies that, in her eyes, silenced dissent and normalized perpetual conflict.

**The Impact of Inaction**

Reflecting on the hardships faced by many Americans during this period, Cher's tone turned deeply empathetic. "We had no help, we had no leadership. There are people in America now that don't even have food; they're losing their homes because the government has given them no money to live on," she lamented. Her critique extended to the broader systemic failures: "If your president doesn't care if you live or die, that's a pretty hard pill to swallow." This sentiment captured the stark realities she observed, inspiring her to champion grassroots efforts for change.

Cher didn't just comment on policy failures; she sought to motivate others, particularly women, to take action. Addressing a rally, she issued a powerful call to arms: "Get your friends and vote. If you don't, you will not recognize this country." Cher's words carried the weight of her personal experiences and historical knowledge. "I remember a time when women didn't have freedom," she told her audience, emphasizing the need to protect and expand rights that were hard-won.

**A Personal War Against Division**: Cher's disdain for divisive leadership was palpable. "This man [Trump] made people that just disagree enemies," she declared. Her aversion to Trump's politics was so strong that she admitted, "I couldn't be friends with someone who voted for him. If I had a husband, I'd leave him." Her candidness underscored her belief in the moral urgency of the moment.

At a personal and national level, Cher viewed Trump's presidency as a turning point. "I've lived through 12 presidents," she reflected, "and never once did I dream there would be one through arrogance and ignorance who could change the face of our world." The stakes, for her, were existential. "We needed to make a curve in a better direction, to create a bond between people. Instead, he separated us more."

**The Euphoria of Obama's Election**
Cher's political activism was not limited to moments of despair. She celebrated victories with equal fervor, recalling Barack Obama's inauguration as one of her life's highlights.

"We were strangers dancing all around Washington, delighted and giddy," she reminisced. Yet, even in that joyous moment, she acknowledged the undercurrents of division. "There was another group of people that felt the same way about Barack Obama as I feel about Trump. They weren't happy; they weren't joyous."

This realization hit her particularly hard while campaigning for Hillary Clinton. A chilling encounter during a campaign stop underscored the depth of the nation's divide. "There were pickup trucks with Confederate flags, and men in camouflage with AK-47s shooting at posts. They told a journalist, 'We're preparing in case Hillary wins.'" The memory haunted her, foreshadowing the turbulent years ahead.

### Living Through the Trump Era

Cher's disdain for Trump extended beyond policy disagreements. For her, his presidency represented an erosion of core American values. "I never thought there would be a president that wouldn't care, that doesn't even like Americans," she said. She accused Trump of fostering chaos and division, describing his actions as "symbolically burning the house down."

Despite her despair, Cher found moments of hope in collective action. Recalling the protests that followed Clinton's defeat, she said, "I was in a depression, but when I saw thousands marching down the street, I got caught up. It took me out of my sadness."

**The Path Forward**

Cher's reflections on leadership offered a contrast between Trump and Joe Biden. She described Biden as a seasoned, empathetic leader with the experience to heal a fractured nation. "I've known Joe since 2006. He's smart, strong, and has a little temper," she said with a wry smile. Her belief in Biden's capacity to unite the country was unwavering.

Looking ahead, Cher emphasized the power of anger as a catalyst for change. "Sadness and depression won't help us. Anger will." Her call to action was grounded in her belief in the resilience of the American people. "The power of the people is bigger than those losers trying to ruin everything."

**Cher's Enduring Legacy**

Throughout her career, Cher has used her platform not just to entertain but to challenge and inspire. Her political engagement, especially during moments of national crisis, reflects her deep commitment to justice and equality. Whether celebrating progress or mourning setbacks, she has remained a passionate advocate for a better future.

Her parting words encapsulate her unwavering determination: "I don't care about him [Trump] at all. What I care about is what we can do to make things right. And we will." Cher's voice, as defiant as ever, continues to resonate in a world that needs it most.

# Chapter Six

**More Humanitarian Works (The Elephant)**

In 2020, as the world grappled with the COVID-19 pandemic, Cher's humanitarian focus shifted to an unexpected cause thousands of miles away from her home. It all began with her discovery of Kaavan, an elephant dubbed "the loneliest elephant in the world," languishing in captivity in Islamabad, Pakistan. Kaavan's plight touched hearts globally, but it was Cher's determined involvement that changed his destiny.

She remembered how it all began: "I started seeing messages from youngsters on my X feed, all saying 'Free the Elephant,' and there was a picture attached." At first, she dismissed it, thinking, "How am I supposed to go to Pakistan and rescue it?" But the sheer number of messages kept growing, and she felt compelled to do something about it. Eventually, the call for action became impossible to ignore, pushing her to take the necessary steps to help the elephant.

## The Call for Help

Cher remembered a conversation she had a year earlier with a man in Qatar who had facilitated the relocation of over 300 elephants to sanctuaries across Africa. She reached out. "I called him and said, 'Hi, you probably won't remember me, but I need to try and move an elephant from Pakistan to a sanctuary.'" To her surprise, he immediately responded, "Great, I'll go."

Within days, the man was on a plane to Pakistan. He assessed the dire conditions Kaavan endured at the Islamabad Zoo. "He told them to put a covering over the shed, take off his shackles, put water in that little pool, and get him some toys," Cher explained. The zoo complied, but the battle to free Kaavan was far from over.

**The Long Road to Freedom**

For years, Cher and her organization, Free the Wild, worked tirelessly through legal and bureaucratic hurdles. "We were in the Supreme Court for a while," Cher noted. Pakistan's Prime Minister, Imran Khan, became a critical ally in the fight. "When Khan said it was a good idea, that helped us unbelievably," she added.

Kaavan's condition was heartbreaking. Years of isolation and abuse had left him severely traumatized. "When elephants are traumatized, they rock back and forth to help themselves feel better, to release endorphins," Cher explained. Witnessing Kaavan's incessant rocking broke her heart. However, a turning point came when Dr. Amir, a veterinarian from Free the Wild, formed a bond with the distressed elephant.

"Dr. Amir got really friendly with him, even though Kaavan kept rocking," Cher shared. "He would bathe him and sing—though it was a really bad version of 'I Did It My Way.'" Despite the circumstances, this small connection offered hope that Kaavan could adapt to a new life.

**The Collaboration with Four Paws**

Realizing the scope of the challenge, Free the Wild partnered with Four Paws, an international animal welfare organization with expertise in relocating animals. The collaboration was monumental. "Four Paws has doctors and resources we needed," Cher explained. Together, the teams orchestrated Kaavan's relocation, addressing every logistical and medical concern.

Kaavan's health required immediate attention. Years of malnutrition and inactivity had taken a toll. To prepare him for transport, he had to lose significant weight. "He lost, like, half a ton, an unbelievable amount," Cher said, emphasizing the meticulous planning required to ensure his safety.

## The Journey of a Lifetime

Transporting Kaavan to Cambodia, where a sanctuary awaited, was a monumental task. He traveled in a specially designed cage, both for his safety and comfort. "They gave him a little sedative—not enough to knock him out, but just to keep him calm," Cher recalled. "He was still completely coherent, and they kept feeding him and talking to him throughout the journey."

Cher flew to Cambodia ahead of Kaavan's arrival. "We landed first and waited for him," she recounted. Upon his arrival, she was overcome with emotion. "It was amazing to see him finally free." The final leg of the journey involved a five-hour drive on a flatbed truck to the sanctuary. Despite the arduous trip, Kaavan's resilience shone through.

**A New Beginning**

At the sanctuary, Kaavan experienced freedom for the first time in decades. The transformation was almost immediate. "He stepped into the sanctuary and started exploring," Cher said, her voice filled with pride. Kaavan's recovery was a testament to the power of compassion and perseverance.

Reflecting on her role, Cher humbly downplayed her efforts. "I love animals, but I love people too," she said. "You have to spread it all around." Her commitment to Kaavan's rescue highlighted her belief in using her platform to make a difference, no matter how daunting the challenge.

**A Legacy of Compassion**: Kaavan's story captured the world's attention, becoming a symbol of hope and the impact of collective action. Cher's involvement transcended celebrity activism; it was a deeply personal mission driven by empathy and determination. Her efforts reminded the world of the importance of standing up for those who cannot fight for themselves.

This chapter of Cher's life exemplifies her enduring legacy as a humanitarian. While she is celebrated for her achievements in music and film, her work with Free the Wild showcases a different facet of her influence—one rooted in advocacy and compassion.

As Kaavan settled into his new home, Cher reflected on the journey. "I didn't think it was possible at first," she admitted. "But sometimes, you just have to take that leap and believe it can be done." Her words, much like her actions, continue to inspire a generation to dream bigger and fight harder for what matters.

Kaavan's rescue was more than a victory for animal rights—it was a core proof of the power of hope, perseverance, and the unyielding belief that change is always possible. Cher's advocacy for Kaavan stands as a shining example of how one person's determination can transform lives, reminding us all of the boundless potential of compassion.

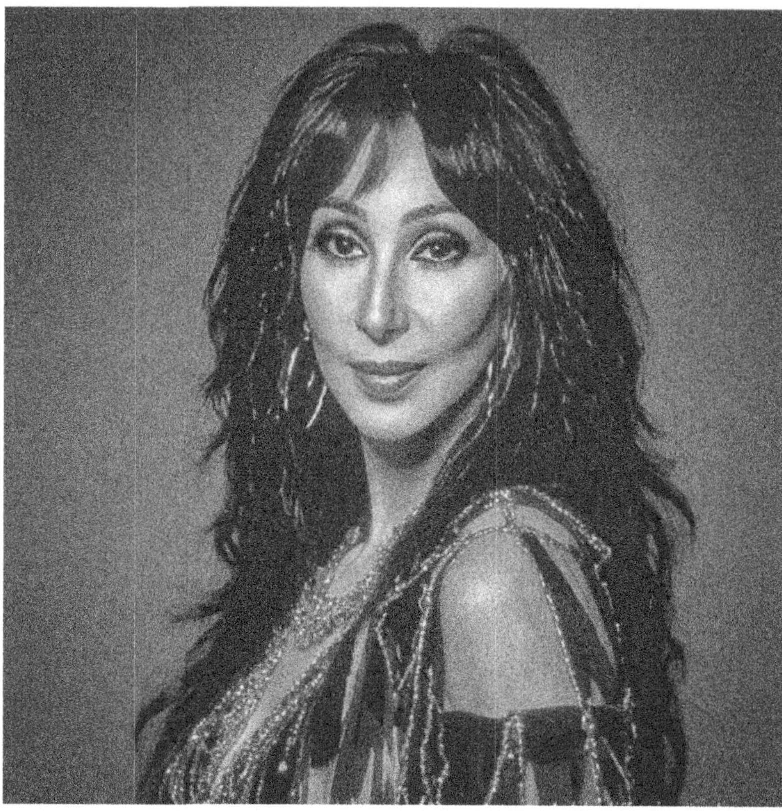

*The End*

Dear Readers,

Thank you sincerely for choosing to purchase a copy of this work. It brings me immense joy to know that my words have resonated with you and, in some way, contributed to your journey.

If you've enjoyed this book, I kindly invite you to share your thoughts by leaving a comment and spreading the word to others. Your support plays a vital role in amplifying this message and means more to me than I can express.

If, for any reason, this work did not meet your expectations, please accept my heartfelt apologies. I am committed to learning, growing, and striving for excellence in all my future endeavors.

Above all, I hope this book reminds you of your value and significance. Your decision to engage with this work reaffirms the connection we share, and I am deeply grateful for your trust.

Thank you once again for your support and for being an integral part of this journey.

[Sekani Jakes]

Made in United States
North Haven, CT
03 December 2024